Formality

Life Beyond the Velvet Ropes

J. D. Stewart

ISBN - 13: 978-1537681177
ISBN - 10: 1537681176

Table of Contents

The modern city is ugly not because it is a city but because it is not enough of a city, because it is a jungle, because it is confused and anarchic, and surging with selfish and materialistic energies.

> – *The Way to the Stars*, *Lunacy and Letters,* G. K. Chesterton

Introduction

The people we see on the red carpet between the velvet ropes come from a variety of walks of life having done something particularly noteworthy. They are seen on television, in the newspapers and on the silver screen. They want to be idolized and often abhor the close up attention that fans gain by violating the celebrity realm. Crashing the class identified region between the ropes, or even demanding autographs on the street fans sometimes insinuate themselves into the world of the celebrity.

Celebrities walk the red carpet between the velvet ropes which keeps them from having to get close to the public, ordinary people. If everyone had Warhol's fifteen minutes of fame at the same time, there would be no one to idolize and worship. Everyone would be the same: no one would enjoy having greater celebrity. But imagine a truly special person, one living outside the velvet ropes and the red carpet and not caring for the bright lights, he or she would be the one living a life dedicated to developing special abilities with potentially admirable grace and an altruistic persona, for a life of exemplary character.

The truth is, that as non-celebrities, we make ourselves special not by what we appear to be but by what we do that marks us as caring and grateful in the real world and in ordinary life styles. In contrast, going far beyond normal existence, celebrity conjures the obdurate haughtiness induced by and for the velvet ropes.

Character is not a requirement for celebrity nor is a caring and self-sacrificial persona. As a newscaster averred several decades ago, and his words have come haunt us: Today we are concerned about celebrity not character. One can be famous without being desirably charming, winsome or concerned about others. A murderer can find a place metaphorically on the celebrity carpet between the velvet ropes, and a criminal can steal public office for celebrity rather than by truth and honor.

Most of us have a long way to go to become people of character. We are potentially an elite and caring species inside the cage of freedom we call civilization. There are and have been barbarians over time, including our era, and the term civilization may have become, in their wake, pejorative. In a barbarian's mind, what was barbaric was not only acceptable, it was their job. When, to the barbarian of old, the cultured and civilized were merely easy to topple, to rob, kill and rape. Today most people would deplore such viciousness, and, if they were themselves barbaric, they would cover up their activities as best they could, or at least spin a new story to counter the truth about themselves. Civilized people have ways of distinguishing themselves other than killing and mimicking the vicious and violent, as an entry into the velvet ropes. Do not these horrible characteristics consist in fact of the totality of undesirable acts and attitudes that make us today the modern example of Attila and his Huns? Or are there more positive characteristics that help identify those that live the better life and distance themselves from the violence and abuse around them? We do not become a formal people by keeping our noses clean and giving to green project write-offs and for the police staying away from violence only leaves us unprotected. If these fabricated concerns sound reasonable then we are part of the dehumanizing barbarism that often fills the velvet ropes. Celebrities do not just star in movies, for example, but bring idealistic cover for their all too often empty and raw lives. They are not formality's home. They are with disdain and condescension opposed to normal caring and common formality in life.

Neutrality does not create formality of life. Many people are not violent and rapacious but live on the edge of civilization. These marginalized people may be law abiding citizens who require little of life and are not active participants in the proffering of an uplifting civilization and are not admirers of higher culture. They live neutral lives, lives not given to forceful direction nor salvaging some piece of society from common belief and action. In general the overall effect in culture that is kindled in most communities is an agreeable politeness and distant coexistence. These are not barbarisms, but they do set the bar much lower if the extent is merely that of cultural pleasantries.

There is a higher cultural milieu that is a function of personal determination with the good of society at its heart. The term that is used here is formalization, the process of higher touch. To those that have little to offer except their numbers, formalization of life may be seen as gilding the lily. What could possibly add to life that could drive mankind to greater societal advantage? The argument against such a higher-brow extension to life may be that not everyone must love opera, champagne, or the theater. These are only some of the more visible options of higher culture and are not the required characteristics but merely some of the possible outer manifestations of formalized life.

As we shall see, formalizing of culture is actually the formalizing of the individual within the communal context. A higher form of discipline is only necessary when we live in and for our chosen group. The wanton grasping of get and take is not only defeated by formality, but is given a love for the group and it prospering.

Formalizing in itself is not an expendable commodity but an expanding cultivation of our most rich and intricate living. It is not the small effects that defines the higher life but the resultant embellishment of all of life's grander functions. It is very difficult, however, to read any support for formalization, which is usually seen as superficial and rote and not a framework for building life's values and actions.

There is an attempt in this book at uncovering formalizing effects while only suggesting formalizing factors. The deeper meaning of civilized formalization may at times serve to address affectations rather than the essence of formalization. On your own you may find some if not all of my given offerings possibly contentious and unworthy. You are encouraged to eliminate some and add others. For these ideas are not to be seen as a guide to perfect living but as additions to broadening of life itself, a deeper and more meaningful life.

Chapter 1

Form, Formality and Fidelity

We all need to feel that we are connected to humanity. A sadness may comes over us when in reading the paper we learn that a child has been intentionally harmed. The right seems to be on our side claiming that killing is too good for the perpetrator. Our indignation goes to retribution very quickly. Our form and formality of response to the atrocity is secondary and fairly standard across the breadth of all that we know of the despicable event. The form is not a primary response of registering the offense against deeply held values, but is jumping to judgement against one who would ostensibly injure a child. Even statements like," killing is too good for him (or her)," even overtones of reciprocating violence toward the abusing party, is not beyond what we believe to be appropriate and justifiable even if by our own hand or the hands of a vigilante group.

We are the "reality society" who believe that most of life's situations require swift and profound retaliation. We draw from television a sense of righteous anger that justifies our feelings which are ramped up by clever producers and directors. Our feelings are heightened by the shows of which we cannot get enough. The artificial scripting of dire circumstance and angry completion drive us to the edge of arm-chair warfare.

This form of feeling, responding with moral outrage is incomplete, markedly fallible and contrived off of a television format by which we gain our insight into good and evil. The justification for such considerations of violence are drawn from one's own mind and heart without finding the innate, inhering and deep-seated hold of unquestionable propriety. Dissolutions of inappropriate emergent character flaws, only falsely wraps one in a cloak of justice.

It may later be found that the abuser did not mean to hurt the child but inadvertently injured, or that the perpetrator had a mental illness and was only slightly older than the child. The law would possibly come in under your degree of harsh penalty finding the mentally ill person had no sense of the dangerous and evil motives and no malice of intent, or that the injure was an unavoidable accident.

The formality of assuaging judgment in the hands of legal authority may be far less stern than your wish for swift and even terminal judgment. Here the formality of legal authority followed the prescriptive and step-wise process of prosecution which could and possibly should find the mentally ill person not guilty or the injury an accident. The form of justice sought by the authorities may be more balanced and less emotionally rendered than your would-be quick and sure justice. The authorities may find that the perpetrator as well as the injured child must be protected and given eleemosynary care. Formality is not an option in thought to judge heinous crimes. It is the better willed judgment based on the weighing of information and evidence among the citizenry and a heart that measures compassion over rigorous and blind action.

Fidelity may seem a strange word to use in referring to the action of moral and ethical judgments. We normally think of fidelity as someone being faithful to another, or loyalty, even dependability. Fidelity to oneself, rather one's innate and inhering values may also be seen in this term - being true to the character that should be grown to indwell us and should be found in our actions. This truth, however, may be only represented by a cicatrix over once inbred lore that grows with time and soul-searching.

This fidelity to truth and character is the basal disposition of those grown sensitive to a dubious justice that echoes from small, hard hearts. The form that this quality of life assumes is critical to a democratic existence. There is no way that any topic found essential to the individual is not also critical to society. If we are not bound by a common communal compassion of character, then we will enjoin society in creating a culture of willful disregard for character, courage and compassion. Form is the scaffolding for what will be argued in the remainder of the book. Content of character is only possible within the right form or formality of life. Fidelity begins in enculturation possibly and grows or is crowded out by the weeds of expediency. Form gives the basic structure for a dependable meaningful life process. Read on to see some of the qualities suggested for content that should fill the essentialism of life.

Chapter 2

Order and Originality

An individual's internal order recognizes inputs or neural penetrations as either eliciting appropriate or inappropriate responses in a sort of self-selecting guidance system. For instance you see someone killed and you are horrified. Your native response maybe disgust or fear, but that may be changing in the modern psyche. Normally one's deepest beliefs and values filter existential events, but a challenge to one's essential self, beliefs and values not vetted properly or at all, may result in assuming misappropriate ends.

The O.J. Simpson trial was seen for some as a sanction against white privilege. Murder got overlooked for a lesser judgment against a potentially cold blooded murderer. In the minds of the jurors there was something, in their own order of recognition and compliance that had been manipulated and was registering racism, which in conflicting and unparalleled importance, took precedence over taking someone's life. Racism is horrible, but one may withstand and survive racism but not murder. These were not thought to be remotely and dimensionally similar before the

O. J. trial. The innate response against murder was a lateral replacement of racism such that a much more serious accusation was over shadowed. The reaction to murder was found less relevant than race by people who had a jaded and subjective view of right and wrong. In substitution of racism for a much more heinous event, personal form was compromised and reordered. The natural response to anyone's murder was made to claim rather that black lives matter to the exclusion of all life matters. More importantly the form or formality of life may have been stripped of its co-dependency among values leaving a skewed imbalance in which great distortion could leave judgment unresponsive to reasonable claims of justice and parity.

In this election year climate, one presidential candidate is willing to steal from the rich and give it to the poor. At first this may seem galant, heroic, but the rich are the people that do business that funds the salaries of the poorer workers. In many cases most people might not want to take on producing a business for all the paperwork, promises of medical coverage, or retirement benefits, in short all the headaches incumbent on owners of businesses. Income equality has become the replacement response for stealing from those that take all the chances with their money and their lives. Where equal pay was once a goal of equality, now it is a justification for theft from those that took the risk of business failure. A socialist or Marxist view would give all consideration to the workers and none to the bosses who provide the jobs. Of course government should take over the care of the worker and the bosses' businesses. Individual ownership may be seen a theft in order to empower the poor at the expense of those who generated all the money. As Margaret Thatcher so cleverly remarked: Socialism works well until the government runs out of other people's money. People insisting on compromising the truth or destroying business are generally unable to come to grips with reasoned understanding that guards against injustice or theft.

Murder and theft once were at least near the top of offenses and registered consistent responses throughout democratic humanity, but that has all changed. Murder of the proper victims may even get you to Paradise with sexual privileges. For some have decided on murder and a promised reward of virgins.

Before disordering our moral compass we were willing to embrace the humdrum of repetition and mundanity in order to guard the given knowns. The living with clear visions of right and wrong opened our minds to new horizons of thought and new ideas, originality, valued in man's progress.

Now we are threatened by atavistic pronouncements of killing and world domination, where are the order of life, the beneficial ideas and peaceful plans for the future?

The human order has been disrupted to promote small and parochial ends for the few. If order is innate to humans, and I believe most would hold to this, then to reduce an ability of most to chaos and fear and even prejudice, is not inappropriate. Our environment dictates our needs for order and a small enclave of warriors committing killings for a fear-mongering god is abjectly wrong.

The real order of one's life is the first attachment to a balanced scaffolding of form and formality. It is a personal redoubt for ongoing forays into the battle of discovery. Order allows us to move ahead intelligently in our lives discovering better paths on our own and not that provided by intimidation, terror or hatred from outside of our purview.

The growth of form and order in one's life promises a future of challenges and a thoughtful walk. It is the structure of one's life that allows innovation and discovery. The adventurist can step outside the normal walk of life in order for neophyte discovery to uncover new dimensions interspersed among the vast assumptions of modernity. New views of ourselves and the world may be uncovered among the prejudices of the present, but large changes in the relative order of life's values and beliefs should raise a red flag especially during existential warfare with one's inner foundational essential selves. Order makes understandable and permits scalable comparisons of events and outcomes. Order determines primacy and is the intermediary agent for our values and beliefs in organizing and valuing. In the scaffolding of form, order and originality bring the newness and expansion of characteristics to build formality.

Chapter 3

Reason and Rigor

Our ability to take a rational path through life is a defining quality of mankind. Furthermore the planning and designing for want or need shows the greatness of man's ideation. From the caves to mansions man has seen the value of form with salient goals and yet with panache. A few of the modifiers that are possible because of reason are style in design, coordination and collaboration of interests, art, science and engineering.

One of the areas in which young people are weak is in following logical thought in a stepwise progression. To move from one step to the next is a sign of power in reason. My goal as a teacher when possible was to draw out facts into detailed and interlocking proofs. Algebra may have given most good students good grades but Geometry proofs measured the mathematical field for reason. Those that had formal thought did well in theorems and corollaries. Logical thought requires a rigorous following of points and positions in argument enabling analysis and synthesis in new directions of learning.

Order is not achievable without reason. There is not a self-ordering system of formality in personal identity. Enculturation by parents from birth and acculturation by ideas on our own, we analyze for suitability of those early values bombarded by a great barrage of ideas, philosophies and temptations. Reason is the ongoing choice of positions and attitudes throughout one's life, not just what we inherited but the equilibrium between what we were taught as children and the ongoing inveigle and analysis of the world and its ideas around you.

Order works to formalized reasoned personalities to inner consistency. Freedom from reason and logic, the bolstering of illogicality, results in conflict in essential beliefs and is grown in personalities that choose actions of pleasure and personal advantage over hard fact and the implications of unsullied communal values within a spirit of self-determination. Ideas can ideally become consistent by obduracy in wise judgment unceasingly.

There is a rigor in reason that cannot endure conflict and inconsistency. Reason dismisses non-unifiable propositions for those that meet all order able requirements. Structured ordering will not permit the lateral equivalence of murder and racism. If racism were ubiquitous, still all would not have to die.

Reason counsels that levels of concern cannot cross orders thereby destroying understanding. As bad as racism is, a dreadful drain on community and human value, it is not from the higher order of considerations of murder and death.

Chapter 4

Meaning and Mastery

In order to know one must see causation, the connection between cause and effect. David Hume claimed that we could not know for certain. We trust some imagined connection between a lineage of facts, none connected but assumed causative of other facts when actually all facts just a laundry list of observables, consistent and coincident. In trying to defeat Hume, Kant caused the same problem of uncertainty by his synthetic *a priori* which claims that things are as they are but when we internalize our experience or observation we filter information through our brains and individualize our perceptions. Dewey was more direct the he averred that by holding a smoking gun, seen pointed at the victim and the whole of the event seen with one's eyes, it would be hard to pronounce certainty of guilt.

The final nail in the coffin by philosophy was hammered into place by Foucault who saw the search for understanding and meaning as a function of history and time. What we accept today is to being altered by time in events, history, and meaning has no permanence and there is no necessary carryover to others and to other communities and countries. Even one person's perception is potentially in perpetual flux.

How is it possible to take Foucault's idea of understanding and rationality and find meaning in life? The answer is that one must maintain a formalized existence in a well grounded and a logically satisfying persona. Uncertainty offers no real answers to the world around you, to no one. One must find the reality of one's place in the functional and collective world in your immediate world and beyond. Without common meaning among humans, without common activities in which all participants are seriously given to meaningful goals, life is unsustainable in a purposeful sense.

We must come to find a workable mastery of the world in which we live. Knowing only a little has given us "on demand production." Everybody knows their part of the production procedure which is called on when needed. Each procedure rises or falls on every parts interdependence, on each and every part, but in the over production method one does not have the total view of production. Production rates may soar when needed and fall when not needed.

Mastery does not mean that one has mastered everything. that would be impossible. To master something manageable is important to knowing your abilities and your weaknesses. To produce something of value for yourself and others builds confidence and your value to others.

My view of learning is not popular today. Mastery was the goal for high school students when I was teaching, but the better goal is to have a broader view of the subject than can be garnered from memory of the facts, although facts are indeed a critical part of learning (see my books on education: *A Teacher's Primer, On Being a Better Teacher,* and *Education of the Mind,* and the composite of all three books *The Teaching Trilogy*).

Mastery has more to do with knowing your way around a discussion of the facts than merely facts alone. Mastery as a process is, however, much more than academic learning. Mastery of one's life precludes knowing all about your house, car and family matters, but rather a way of seeing these important issues as an ongoing and interacting group of considerations. A better way of seeing mastery, in this sense, is to balance all important issues such that all get appropriate attention when needed, as needed.

A person who can bring solution to the integrated problem that develops among issues and people for which one has authority or responsibility, even if not absolute responsibility, is a person who is approaching the problem of mastery in a mature way, and is striving to protect and potentiate the interaction of responsibilities among those that need to be in consideration.

Who can say they have mastered life? Possibly only those who left their futures to knowing factually, never stepping into the quagmire of flux that requires not a hard understanding but one with which we must move on less than intrinsic knowledge to capture a transient knowledge of the way the world is in a process of constant change. Mastery does not mean that change can occur in your guiding credos but in the way you see the relationships among events and outcomes interpreted by those hard and inflexible values and beliefs..

Chapter 5

Accessibility and Accord

I once had a brilliant student who taught me in every lesson that I taught him. He was a brilliant person, but he had a problem with intimacy. The problem did not arise from his genius, but that he wished that all relationships were objective like the one he had with computers. Unlike with people computer information is stored in a form that is accessible to the right codified entry input. This was clean, easy for him, and the range of information was seemingly unlimited.

Many times he and I discussed his tendency to learn without having to develop relationships. He graduated at the end our year together receiving the highest scholarship from his chosen university. I wrote two single-spaced pages for his application information, and never needed that much writing to tell of someone's worth for academics. He was a special student. The most brilliant and gifted learner I had ever had the honor to teach. Before he finished college, he had an experiment on the shuttle. He soon got married and had many children. He also became a guarded secret for Uncle Sam as an engineer.

This young man was so smart that he finally saw the wisdom of relationships, and for many years he would send me a Christmas letter telling of the family activities and a short and general tidbit about his secret job description. The most important thing ended up being the family relationships he now highly valued, it would appear, above all digital truth.

Glorification of 0s and 1s was replaced by his accessibility to his family and his family's accessibility to him in his innermost and concerned self. The evidence of his large family and the details about all members of his family showed a mature husband with invaluable ties to his family.

Relationships are not alway good, and some may prove exhausting if not fraught with danger. Accessibility opens one up to vulnerability to being taken advantage of and hurt. The person that is accessible must know of the potential for harm, yet must find the courage to risk one's deepest and most hardily guarded values and beliefs, for beliefs and values short of sacrificing who one is, is going to far in pursuit of helping others. The purpose of this sacrificial openness is to go more than halfway to securing relationships even in vitriolic relationships. The purpose is to breed accord among those who would attack you personally and unceasingly. Attacks on the inner man may be hurtful and discouraging but leaves the open heart knowing that all has been risked for the hope of accord. This must not compromise the essentialist inner life of value and beliefs, and should only be practiced when appropriate among people one knows well and definitely not organizations of people where diatribe may drive relationships among the membership.

Chapter 6

Likability and Love

Generally people will agree about a particular person being affable. When a deeper appreciation is considered true character tends to surface. The classroom dynamic comes to mind when I think of likable students in my teaching experience. With many students interacting and sharing information in group projects, the individual personalities can often be seen quite clearly. Often the best liked students are not those so judged by teachers. When some students are challenged by the teacher or even other students, their likable facades are lost due to competition or even basic territorial issues concerning friendships and group control.

I once had a student who was very quiet, did her work, and was a good student. She disappeared from class never to return. There was no drop paperwork. She just did not show up again. When I asked the administrators what had happened to her, they were mute. Through the grapevine, I learned that she was hearing voices and was evaluated for paranoiac schizophrenia and had been placed in guarded care. Anyone in her class would have thought her incapable of doing those things the voices demanded from her. Yet experience has shown that those voice, no matter how desperately opposed, without proper medications will in some way direct the hearer's actions. It is just as well that we did not see deeper into her personality, we would not have believed her to be so fragile and potentially dangerous.

One of my student was voted most friendly as a senior which is in spite of the fact that he was an evangelical Christian who asked everyone he talked to if they knew Jesus. Although this might be a threatening inquiry from another student, fellow students saw that his questioning was not interrogation but that he had a true interest in them. He went out of his comfort zone to inquire about them. The students saw deeply into his heart and determined his positive motivation, and found him likable.

So what makes a person lovable? What drives personality preference beyond liking to loving? Knowing you hold another to a higher standard of trust and truthfulness, the kind of person you would trust with your life still does not necessarily mean that this person must evoke a feeling of love.

Once in a conversation with a friend, a teaching colleague, the question arose about love. This young woman wanted to get married, and thought that, for some strange reason, I might be able to define or clarify the term. How would she know if she found the right person? Immediate my answer turned from the metaphysics of relationships to praxis. For no matter what love was at its theoretical core, its application was not only its goal but elicited its manifestation. I told my dear friend, and was reminded of my answer a decade and a half later - love is letting one's lover win.

Love is not a completion, despite the fact that two people in love may be quite competitive personalities. To subjugate one's reflexive disposition to win to another is the ultimate trust in someone else. At the highest level of trust and truthfulness love reigns supreme.

The characteristics of persona that allows likability and love of another to be uncompromising and unconditional is only possible when one's own welfare is no more important than any very close other. Likability has little to do with the emission of positive and affable signals to others but is an emptying of oneself for the benefit of others. Although we do not use this term "like" to address the sacrificial work of the armed forces, policemen and firemen, such terms apply as an active characteristic of a dutiful agent of help and protection even when the expression of likability is not forthcoming from all of those involved.

Love of country, of family, are dedications to a standard of faith. Not faith that is undependable, but faith that stands invisible, often unspoken, that has the confidence of those protected, by those that are ultimately dependent. Both likability and love are not just other complements of form or formality but actually bend and bolt together that scaffolding here called formality, which cannot be erected without them. In conforming the scaffolding to one's life, liking and loving allow the introduction of other characteristics of formality.

Chapter 7

Intensity and Ideation

The general view of intensity is that of someone obsessing to the point of personal pathology, one tracked and oblivious, if not summarily dismissive of others and the ideas of others. But a more favorable view of intensity is to hold a thought or a progression of one's thoughts to a conclusion or conclusions. It is foremost the mind penetrating a conundrum bringing critical light and clarity by unclouded reason to a problem of importance.

My experience from the classroom is that teenage students as a group do not give themselves to problems of life and do not pursue difficulties unless they are easily resolveable. Both a reluctance to develop the intensity of holistic thought for an easier way to see the world aided by an educational system that reveres facts over reason is the new paradigm for well-educated graduates.

Factual learning is easier to effect in students' while formalized thought and associated abstract reasoning is harder to communicate to most students. Ideation is the common product of intense thought and has given man the way out of the caves. Great thought has given us such amazing technologies, yet today our most modern and cutting edge technological advantages are for a majority of Americans toys as life organizing time wasters like cell phones. Children can do anything with a phone and do, but they have no knowledge of the inner workings of the technology. It is this superficial understanding of technology that dominates young person's and even older people's lives. They go and do everything punching the buttons on the phone, inattentive to the world they are traversing. Published stories hold that at times phone hypnotized users walk into traffic or fall into bodies of water.

Ideas that have changed our lives for the good have given the easily distracted a shallow pit of diversion in which to wallow or even parish. The reason, if not one of many reasons, is that to not have a phone or not understanding every way in which it can be used, is a mark against who you are. Not knowing its total number of functions: calling, texting, browsing the internet, lighting, checking the weather, means you are no in the proper environment doing the approved phone activities. The list of functions grows with every new app downloaded. Those that are drawn into this lifestyle forfeit the gift of living in a fascinating world outside the digital realm.

That is not to say that there is only intensity of deep thought. Certainly intensity is required to master one's phone, despite the pedestrian levels of accomplishment inherent in the process. Intensity of thought is required to juggle the starting point of purpose, the multi-stepped path chosen and the predetermined terminus of the ideation involved. The hypotheses - tested by greats such as Pasteur, Newton, Einstein, and so many others - are marked by dedication and unflinching attention to the process. No less important in the process is the clarity of observation and the guiding of thought and action through a world of equivocality.

Chapter 8

Theology, Truth and Trust

In reference to his religion, G. K. Chesterton wrote in *What's Wrong with the World* that "The Christian ideal has not been tried and found wanting. It has been found difficult; and left untried." This was one of many writings in which Chesterton held up his trust in the truth of Christianity.

So what is the immediate significance of putting forth the idea of God? In its simplest form the prospect that there is an Almighty draws us to the idea that we have limits and we did not build this world but live in it by the patience, privilege and grace of God. To those who see their lives as sacraments to the world around them, this is a great fashioner of form and formality. Like love it helps shape the scaffolding of our lives on the dependence God on others. If there is a God, then the impact on one's outlook on life is drastically different from one whose form of life answers only to self.

An oath of trust sworn on a Bible is at its foundations a vow of truth. Any oath without the confidence of truth and trust is merely a platform for prosecution, a judgment against a lack of trust and truth. We swear in the jury box. We swear an oath to office. Trust is demanded and truth, as a trueness to our claims, is expected unceasingly. When voted out or impeached, the question of propriety, not just illegality, is leveed against our elected leaders. Drawn against the oath of office is the temptation of wealth and power which clearly disqualifies the elected and appointed leaders, yet the circumspection of risk seems to be the part and parcel of many given our elected trust. But an all-seeing God is not fooled.

Contrary to an orthodox view of faith to God is the modern understanding of a god who set the world in motion and then walked away having no daily function in our lives, a deistic ghost, lost in the ages. However, a God that greets one's rising in the morning and influences one's life with words of care and grace, is a personal God who holds us to a standard high enough for us to procure it, but far from lofty goals unapproachable by man. We are real, flesh and blood and God holds us to what we can do, and helps us to attain that goal as he works a far larger plan of time through eternity

The formality of our lives is drastically affected by God, if we embrace his care and direction. As love reconfigures our form, so belief and sworn dedication to God, the one who can drastically change our form, can alter our goals and our understanding of the world in which we live and of ourselves. Love and yielding to God in trust conforms our person and makes the acquisition of the previously described formality characteristics more easily fashioned and fitted into our persons and personalities.

The one you love is given that love because of trust and truth. Apart from just deciding that one no longer loves another person usually means that there is no longer trust. Truths not a defensible statement of fact in marriage but the lives of those in love with one another.

Chapter 9

Yielding and Yearning

There must be a balance between yielding and yearning. They must remain in tension in order to not drive harder than necessary and not be too docile to stand for beliefs and values. These seemingly conflicting characteristics, assuming that the other characteristics of formality suggested in previous chapters are in place, provide for a suitable temperament for genteel living, gentility without pretentious affectations. The cultural and even the animal instincts must yearn in normal fashion for life. Yearning should be linked to formality balanced functions such as those afore mentioned characteristics. If balance is achieved then the degree of drive that keeps the longing for each day and its adventures will remain appropriately alive throughout life.

Yielding is far more difficult to balance since it must recognize authority at all times, true authority well examined. Compromising any of one's formal characteristics will not only offset good judgment but will fracture the balance of formal scaffolding and leave one open to slippage into self-absorption.

On the other hand, yielding to common hedonistic powers will begin a rapid de-scaffolding and a possible loss of other forms and characteristics of formal living. A pastor that I know who in counseling a your college freshman was asked how he could understand the faith which had been so important to the young man in his youth. The young man was beginning to doubt his purpose in life. The pastor only asked him one question, "How long have you been sleeping with your girl friend?" In this one act of selfishness, in the disregard for her possibly true feelings, he had turned sexual attraction into hedonism, and began to dismantle formalities influence in his life. Yearnings had off balanced yielding, and the potential love for the girl friend had been squandered in noncommittal and stolen pleasure.

If one has no authority to manage one's desires and yearnings, then a formalized life is very unlikely. If desires drive one's life then the formality of life is lost to overloading one's nervous system to passion, which in effect de-scaffolds formality.

Conclusion

Formality, in the sense that it is used here is not an expectation of any course of action, nor a matter of style, rigid convention or etiquette's rule of behavior. For these expectations are seen today as undesirable and unnatural and are considered pessimistic and now entombed in a cultural prejudice that ridicules true character and gains derision when ever the term arises. Those that declaim formality for the benefit of those that still think that life should be civil and should put forward its best face, do more damage to its original intention than all the neophytes that allow the malingering of pseudo-belief to cloud the reputation of formality. Half-hearted espousal of proper character and behavior is the worst agent of infamy of all prosecutions of formality. Such implications are ruined by a wink and nod to those attitudes that steal the uninformed and opaque view of probity, damning right and equivocating on poor behavior.

Form, order, clear reason, real meaning to life, mastery of civilized life, accessible and accord to all civilized people, dedication to intensity and pursuit of great ideas, trust in God and the good, truth, yielding to authority and yearning for a better life for all are hallmarks of the person who stands for and lives life in formality.

Unfortunately we are in an era where winning at all costs is the general rule of self-determination. There is little that is civilized about reality television, and this has set the new mark for personal demeanor. Feeling justified by such overtly aggressive models of behavior goes against every thing that most people learn from parents and teachers. The simple fact is that those people that do not copy the entertainment standard for behavior are always seen as cooperative and pleasant people, yet to some degree these same people that we would love to be around us, may also be seen as pushovers or failures in protecting their interests.

There should be a return to communal values and decency, to the formality that made America and Americans great. The first action is to speak up for understanding and cooperation, when self-interests seem to push others aside with vitriol. Another step would be to show generosity to business relations and friends. Still another action would be to offer time to help those in need. This turn around must start with each of us. An attitude of cooperation will quickly either draw down confrontation or push aggressive people to verbally attack. Being able to take the abuse if necessary is an indication that formalities are being brought to play in your life, which is a good sign. If attacked merely satisfy yourself that others know what they see is right and are convicted of their own shortcomings.

Above all formality is the open expectancy of a good life. Without regrets,with missteps corrected and admitted to, one can live a formal life to the betterment of self and all those for whom you hold sway.